Where's My Zen?

Where's My Zen?

A Parable of the Ten Paradoxes

Master Nomi

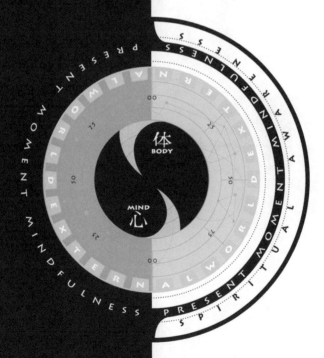

A Journey of Enlightenment and Peak Performance

Where's My Zen?

A Parable of the Ten Paradoxes

Master Nomi

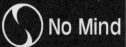 No Mind Publishing Company

Los Angeles, California, U.S.A.
1-877-4NOMIND

First printing 2008.

Printed and Bound in China. Published in the United States of America by No Mind® Publishing Company, 2008, Standard Address Number 256-7423

THE LIBRARY OF CONGRESS HAS CATALOGED THE E-BOOK, PAPERBACK, HARDCOVER, AND DVD AS FOLLOWS:
Master Nomi
Where's My Zen? A Parable of the Ten Paradoxes of No Mind / Master Nomi

No Mind® is a registered trademark of No Mind Publishing Company
Total Mental Fitness® is a registered trademark of No Mind Publishing Company
Awareness is the Only Universal Constant™ is a trademark of No Mind Publishing Company
Where's My Zen?™ is a trademark of No Mind Publishing Company

ISBN 0-938058-04-5 (e-book) (978-0-938058-04-5)
ISBN 0-938058-05-3 (paperback) (978-0-938058-05-2)
ISBN 0-938058-06-1 (hardcover) (978-0-938058-06-9)
ISBN 0-938058-07-X (DVD) (978-0-938058-07-6)

1. Selp-Help 2. Business 3. Sports 4. Spirituality
I. Title

LCCN 2007937817

ATTENTION CORPORATIONS, UNIVERSITIES, COLLEGES, and PROFESSIONAL ORGANIZATIONS: Discounts are available on bulk purchases of this book for educational or gift purposes, or as premiums for increasing magazine subscriptions or renewals. Special books or book excerpts can also be created to fit specific needs. For information, please write to No Mind® Publishing Company, 13351-D Riverside Drive #601, Los Angeles, CA 91423; or call 1-877-4NOMIND.

Dedicated to Chelsea and Allix for
listening to the inspired and sometimes
uninspired wisdom of Master Nomi for so many years.
As they listened to the countless hours of
talking about confusing paradoxes and No Mind,
it suddenly became worth it all, when they said,
"Dad, there is no 'real' answer to *Where's My Zen*?"

And for all those who have yet to uncover the magic and
understanding of finding their own answer.

Many paths lead from the foot of the mountain
But at the peak we all gaze at the
Single bright moon

Ikkyu (1394–1481)

Contents

Zen Attitude

Inspired by the cosmos
Inspired by the natural world
Developed for the human world
Perfection of human-ness
Is the whole as a part;
Potentiality that is inherent
In all those of strong will
All those who pursue the Way;
Seeking liberation
Seeking release from bondage
Seeking one's own destiny
Followers in the Way
Where all masters have passed

Nothing is hidden
In the sacred teachings,
There are no special orders
No esoteric doctrine
No mystical powers
No eternal supremacy;
Nothing to cling to
Only one's determination
In the realization of truth;
Realization of enlightenment
A quite laughable state,
Nonsense riddles all grasped
With all humility of the
accomplishment

There are no sins
Evil is strictly the act of mind,
There are no prayers
Ultimate desire and hope are within,
There are no graces
One must sanctify oneself,
There is no faith
Other than one's own determination,
There are no prophet's words
Attachment to ideas hinder the path,
There is freedom of faith
Yet there remains only doubt
Satori! Now there is no doubt

World religions exist simultaneously
The world created a hundred ways
History has many stories
Wherein lies the absolute truth?
Condemning one condemns another,
"This is truth and that is false"
Exists only as an independent belief;
Absolute truth needs no source
Absolute truth needs no label,
Labels manifest prejudices
And as such are hindrances;
Recognizing truth as truth
Appears as a mystical inner journey

A question of faith
A question of belief
When ones "sees"
Faith and belief disappear;
Yet truth is simple
Found everywhere, yet nowhere
Like dying of thirst
While in a sea of fresh water;
Attitude is thought
Attitude is feelings
Attitude is a state of mind
Zen dispels all attitude
So… Zen attitude is its very absence

by Master Nomi

("Zen Attitude" is one of the 39 insights which are published in No Mind 601 of *The Ten Paradoxes*.)

A Word from Master Nomi

You are invited on a journey of enlightenment and personal growth. Take no baggage. Take no preconceived ideas. Simply be with life as it is in this moment. All I ask is that you have No Mind.

Master Nomi
Los Angeles, 2008

Preface

Where's My Zen?
The Ten Paradoxes of No Mind®

Join Master Nomi as he reveals the Ten Paradoxes to three travelers who, on a journey to find their Zen, mystically encounter the Hut of the Blind Donkey in Japan. This small hilltop monastery where Master Nomi lives serves as the backdrop for an unforgettable night filled with enlightening experiences and ancient Zen secrets.

Through the Ten Paradoxes, Master Nomi reveals that our minds are trained from birth to be overly analytical. We over-think and over-analyze; we feel we must identify and name everything, categorize, and associate to understand how each thing fits into our world. We never objectively perceive reality as it is. We perceive, act, and react as we have been conditioned through a lifetime of environmental and genetic cues. We block our intuitions, inspirations, creativity, psi functions (higher perceptions), and spiritual awareness. As the Master says, we simply lose our Zen and inevitably suffer the consequences. Convinced that we've been taught properly, we assume that any perceived shortcomings are our own personal failures. We think we're just not trying hard enough, so we try harder. Many of us try so hard we become stressed out. We shut down our creative flow and inhibit our natural abilities. Our vision becomes jaded. Our emotions, dulled. Our bodies, tired. We literally worry ourselves sick. We no longer move through life with the fluency and vibrancy of youth. *We lose the play*. We lose the "flow" by over-trying, over-thinking, and over-analyzing everything and everyone. We begin to look for a way to once again find our inner contentment and ponder the question, "Where's my Zen?"

Experiencing your Zen breaks the illusion and limitations of the overly analytical mind, so through No Mind you can experience the mind's full, limitless potential. It liberates your natural, inherent abilities and talents, without effort. It allows you to become aware of a lifetime of conditioning so you can begin to live and experience *unconditional life*—made possible by *knowing where your Zen is.* Only then can you see who you really are, fully express yourself, and attain peak performance. You then live in a new spiritual awareness and discover the full potential of your own mind-body dynamic—the breadth of your natural abilities and talents.

Master Nomi maintains that awareness, liberated from the constraints of your conditioned self, your ego or I-illusion, is then free to flow into all areas of your life—sports, health, business, relationships, spirituality, and academics— leading to reduced stress, peak performance and deep inner contentment. A liberated awareness is the key to realizing enlightenment. We realize through Master Nomi's wisdom that there can be no literal answer to the question, "Where's my Zen?" We can only *experience* it.

We are born enlightened, then we lose it. Now, following the path of No Mind, we can experience it again. So join Master Nomi as he opens the "gateless gate."

Chapter 1: **The Three Travelers**

One day, on a mountain towering high above a Japanese village, there were three young travelers: Mindful, Spirit and Iill (pronounced "ill"). All three were "looking for their Zen." They were strangers to each other, but not to the feeling of inner discontent that had brought them here. It was as though they'd lived their lives in chains and never knew they had the key. They felt trapped in their professions, objectives, and expectations, frustrated in their various attempts to sustain what they ultimately came to believe were unauthentic lives. They lived as they were conditioned to live—the way they believed was the best way to live. But they were merely existing and not living at all. They were trapped in their *mind box* and needed to break free. The three knew that those who have "experienced their Zen" are truly free, develop peak performance, and live with deep contentment through enlightenment.

So although they were from different countries and had never met before, their research and inquiries had led each of them to seek the famous Rinzai Zen Monastery in Japan, which was opening its Zen school to the outside world. The three, eager to look for their Zen, signed up for the next available classes.

The three were quite different in their lives and beliefs. Mindful was a professional athlete from Australia. He thought that being able to answer the question, "where's my Zen?" would allow him to, as many sports psychologists say, "get into the Zone," or attain "peak performance" in his sport. Iill, a businessman from America, enjoyed considerable material success and tried to find happiness by accumulating wealth. Yet he, too, remained ungrounded and apprehensive. Discovering where his Zen is, he hoped, would lead to deep contentment, a greater understanding of people, and to becoming even more productive and excellent in his work. Spirit was from Italy. Her Italian father was a Christian minister and her Russian mother was of Jewish descent. Spirit had become versed in both religions, but even after years of devoted following and worship, she was still left searching. As many others of her generation, she was searching for a "direct experience" of God. It was her great hope and prayer that experiencing her Zen would open the doors to inner peace, spiritual enlightenment and self-realization.

And so, Mindful, Iill and Spirit were on an intense inner journey and hoped that the Rinzai—a uniquely mystical place—would fulfill their expectation of experiencing a rigorous, yet intimate and enriching mental training program.

The three travelers encountered one another for the first time at the airport in Japan while awaiting the private tour bus that would carry them to their destination. Although they'd expected to join a larger group, only the three of them boarded the small bus. Following brief introductions, they were en route to embrace the experience of their lives. At least, that was their hope.

Chapter 2: **The Journey Begins**

As the bus left the airport and headed toward the Rinzai, Mindful, Iill and Spirit spoke of places, people, and things which they had thought would help them discover their Zen. They shared stories of hardship and joy, success and failure, love and romance. Yet, in all of this they agreed that there was still something missing. They had never found the deep happiness, contentment, freedom, or enlightenment that they'd sought. They all agreed that they had always looked for those things outside of themselves. Even though they all took different paths to look for their Zen, they'd never found it. Mindful looked for it through his sports; Iill sought it through money, success, and material things; and Spirit tried to experience it through religion and faith.

Iill had always relied on his calculating mind to make everything work out or add up, just as he always over-analyzed and tried to categorize things and people. He indeed sometimes felt trapped within his own *mind box* of how life should be, at least according to how he perceived it. He often felt the world was against him, and he didn't like that notion at all. He sometimes felt isolated and alone inside of himself. He couldn't shake the feeling that there was more—something more important, more substantial, more significant in life.

For his part, Mindful had achieved a measure of local fame in his sport and, unlike Iill, had searched for and found his Zen through competition. He'd had a brief encounter with a "selfless" feeling of simply *being in the Now*, during which he performed with greater energy and focus than ever before. He experienced the *opposite* of what he'd been taught, which was to *try hard and push yourself harder*. Yet no one, not even his coach, really understood or could ever quite describe this "selfless" feeling. After doing some research, though, Mindful learned that many athletes have felt the same thing, but were incapable of defining it, usually being too embarrassed to even speak of it. He had experienced what many sports psychologists call the *zone* or the *flow,* or *peak performance*. However, Mindful knew that such a feeling went beyond everyday existence—not only because he'd perform so amazingly well in the physical realm, but because he'd also felt somehow spiritually alive. By the same token, the harder he tried to re-create the experience, the more he failed. "There must be another way!" he thought.

As for Spirit, her concerns went beyond the diverse and intoxicating successes of the material life. Her work as a museum curator in Italy led her to appreciate the subtle details of things that most people overlooked. She embraced art and history. Her parents instructed her in the religions of their God, who they believed chooses our path and guides us along the way. She attended Mass and temple and was friends with many of the local townspeople who shared her religious beliefs. She was happy in her life, but knew also that there was something else, somewhere—*in here,* not *out there,* as she'd been taught. She studied the experiences of Christian and Jewish mystics who sought God-consciousness or a "direct experience" of God. These mystics discovered a universal oneness that went deeper than anything she had previously experienced in her religious practices. At this point, Spirit was unsure of much, but certain of one thing: she would not find that *something else* that she was seeking in her home town, but hoped that soon, very soon, at the Rinzai Monastery she would realize this oneness for herself.

All three knew their individual life journeys were only part of their ultimate paths. There was still some secret path or ancient way waiting for them, somewhere *in here,* which would help them discover their Zen and experience happier, more prolific, and spiritually aware lives. They each explored different techniques in confronting and solving the challenges of their lives and what appeared to be mistakes of the past. And yet, maybe those were not mistakes at all; maybe everything transpired as it had because it was the only path they had known. Yet now, it had led them all here.

Iill relied on his great analytical and intellectual power in his approach to life. Mindful used his physical prowess and strength and his knowledge of teamwork. Spirit employed her faith and belief in God as a guide. Sometimes, for each of them, on one level or another, life worked out. Other times, it did not. But all three were looking for a way to see through the ups and downs of life and to see the world in a new, fresh, direct way instead of through their own *mind box* of filtered experiences.

Experiencing their Zen meant getting out of the trap of their mind boxes.

Trapped they were, but only for the moment. They had fallen into comfortable and binding routines, seemingly satisfied with life as it was, but were ultimately left with a feeling that there was something more. Each of them also knew of many other people who were attempting to attain that "something else," all the while struggling with the daily grind or working hard to climb the ladder of success or often just to make ends meet. They knew that their happiness was somewhat conditioned by what they had achieved and what they had acquired. And if they were to lose all of it, they might be very unhappy. Other friends they knew feared they might never achieve success at all. Fear, worry, and anxiety seemed to be common components of their lives.

As the hours passed on the lengthy ride to the monastery, the three travelers became acquainted and began to understand their differences, as well as what made them alike. They were amazed to find that they were all seeking the same objective: to get out of the trap of their mind box and experience something beyond themselves, by finding what Zen masters call the *self-nature,* or what is more commonly known as *spiritual awareness*. They spoke enthusiastically, excited at having found companions for their journey.

"Hey, mate," Mindful said, looking over at Iill. "That's a curious name. Why did your parents name you Iill?"

"Well," Iill replied, "both my parents were psychologists and they named me after the fact that the "I" is an illusion. So it's short for *I-illusion*." He then leaned back, laughed and added, "Funny thing is, I've spent my entire life building up my *I-illusion* and identifying with who 'I' am."

Joining in on the name game, Spirit said, "My name is obvious. My parents were quite religious and my papa, in fact, was a minister."

Suddenly, they were jolted by a loud bang, like a small explosion. "Uh-oh," the bus driver frowned. "That doesn't sound good, I'd better pull over."

As they came to a stop, the three passengers looked around and were awed by the enchanting vista before them. They were on a bluff overlooking a valley of stunning beauty. *Matsu* pine trees densely lined the narrow road on both sides, chasing the mountainside.

Mindful, Iill and Spirit got off the bus as the driver looked under the hood. They gazed across the road and noticed a structure partially hidden among the pines. It appeared to be an old monastery. It was surrounded by a thick stone wall with statues of meditating monks that flanked a heavy wooden gate.

"I'm going to run ahead and get some help," the driver said. "We're still about ten kilometers from your destination. It's better if you stay here until I get back. You will be safe here."

"We can't just stay here by ourselves!" said Iill, alarmed.

"Where are we?" Mindful wondered. "Why don't we go inside that place and ask for help?"

"They say that home has been abandoned," the driver replied. "And I believe those gates have been locked shut for years. I'd better go before it gets dark. Stay in this area and you'll be fine," he added, and hurried down the road.

"Wait!" yelled Iill as the driver disappeared around a bend.

The three were left staring at one another and at their surroundings. Finally, curiosity got the best of them. "This looks like such a spiritual place," Spirit said. "Let's go inside and check it out."

"We can't go in," Iill protested. "That's trespassing."

"Hey, c'mon mates," said Mindful. "If it's locked, we can just jump over the wall and check it out." So with Iill and Spirit behind him, Mindful approached the gate and began to force it open. But no force was necessary. The massive wooden doors swung open easily. "Come on," he said, "let's go inside."

The three ventured into the courtyard, and were surprised to find themselves in a pristinely maintained and landscaped Zen garden, with beautiful large boulders and black and gray gravel. The gravel was raked in parallel lines running along the edge of the courtyard, with concentric circles framing the rock groups. Several shrine lanterns, black pine trees, and bamboo lined the edges of the gravel areas. At the end of the straight path through the garden was a Japanese maple which framed the entrance to what appeared to be an old Japanese temple. They passed through a small alcove, through the open front door, and into a large corridor with an open ceiling and curved natural wood beams. A light flickered down the corridor from one of the rooms.

"I think I see someone," Iill said, a bit startled. "Let's get out of here…now! "No, wait," said Spirit, grabbing Iill by the sleeve. "Let's go in and introduce ourselves. Maybe they can help us."

Chapter 3: **The Meeting**

The three walked cautiously through the dimly lit corridor toward the room. Along the way, they passed ten painted pictures illustrating what looked like someone searching for an ox and then taming it. Toward the end of the series was a simple painted circle and a landscape scene. Below these were a series of nine finely drawn circular images that appeared to be an ancient compass with a star map. As they entered the room, they discovered a man seated on a pillow, writing with an ink brush. Surrounding him were ten scrolls, which appeared to be written in ancient Japanese calligraphy, all beautifully framed and preserved. At the center of a table, encased in glass, rested an extremely weathered stone with carvings on it—intricate circles with two Japanese characters, English notations and a design that resembled an ancient star map.

"I have been expecting you." the old man said, his eyes still focused on his brush.

"What do you mean?" asked Mindful. "Who are you?"

"Sorry for the intrusion," Spirit said to the old man, "We're on the way to the Rinzai Zen Monastery just down the road, but our bus got stuck out front, and our driver went for help. We were looking for somewhere safe to wait. My name is Spirit. And this is Mindful, and this is Iill."

The old man stopped writing and, looking directly at his three visitors for the first time, stood up and bowed. "My name is Master Nomi," he said, pronouncing it *know-me.* "I knew that soon more travelers would come to learn the Ten Paradoxes and the Secrets of No Mind and take them back to the world to help others."

"Excuse me?" Iill said, totally confused. "The Ten Paradoxes? No Mind? I don't have a clue what you're talking about." Spirit motioned for Iill to stop speaking. "Perhaps this is fate or destiny," she said. "Perhaps we have been guided here."

"By whom?" Iill wondered. "God? I suppose you really believe that, don't you? Well, I don't think so. To me, this is just the bus driver's incompetence for not being prepared."

As though he hadn't heard a word of the debate, Master Nomi continued. "This temple is called the Hut of the Blind Donkey, and I am one of the few remaining Crazy Clouds."

"Um, excuse me, mate," Mindful interrupted. "But what exactly is a Crazy Cloud?"

"The Crazy Clouds are the nonconformist Zen masters," Master Nomi explained, "often disguised as beggars, preachers, or madmen. At first they appear as rebels or radicals, but in fact they are enlightened masters with deep understanding. The name *Nomi* is short for *No Mind,* as I knew you would ask me."

The Master walked toward the scrolls on the wall. "When the mind is clear," he continued, "we see the subtle intuitions that come to us. When the mind is cloudy, we see only the clouds. In a clear pond we can see *through* the water to its bottom. In a cloudy pond, we see only the surface of the water. Others have come before you and learned. Was it their fate that brought them here? Perhaps. Perhaps, in many ways, we are guided by the forces and flow of nature, and destiny may simply be the results or end products of that process. But the results relate to time, and at every moment of time, a new destiny may materialize. So you see, all things are relative."

"Aye," said Mindful in amazement. "I agree. We're headed to the Rinzai to take classes in order to discover where our Zen is. Iill is from the States, Spirit is Italian, and I'm an Aussie." He turned to his new friends and said, "Hey, mates, I think we found our Master." Then he asked, "What's that stone on the table?"

"Many years ago," the Master replied, "I discovered the stone while working as a carpenter in Shikoku on the demolition of a very old Japanese temple in the city. It was hidden under the floorboards with the scrolls and other stone fragments. It has taken 25 years of my life to decipher the stone and understand these scrolls. I have learned that they represent the Ten Paradoxes and the Secrets of No Mind—a path to achieving inner peak performance and enlightenment.

"Wow!" Iill exclaimed. "That's quite a story. You've done all this work. Why don't you publish it and get the word out? There are lots of people trying to find their Zen."

"Find their Zen?" Master Nomi chuckled. "You will only be able to know where your Zen is when you no longer look for it. The more you look, the more it escapes you. Your Zen is with you always. But as the cloudy water, you cannot see it until you learn to clear your mind. When you learn to see *through* yourself, then your Zen will emerge like an emerald glimmering in the sandy bottom of the pond. This is called *No Mind*. It is not the water, the bottom of the pool, or the emerald. It is the glimmer itself shining through it all."

Chapter 4:
Paradox One

Master Nomi pointed to the first scroll on the wall. "This is the First Paradox:

ACT. REACT.
BUT NEVER TRY.

Mindful was puzzled. "That makes no sense to me," he said. "I've always been taught to try hard, to keep trying and never give up."

"That's right," Iill agreed. "In order to succeed, you have to give it your all. Otherwise, you won't make it in life. As for me, I've always worked hard in order to be successful. And it's paid off."

Spirit said, "I think Master Nomi is talking about letting go, and letting God or the universe guide you."

"Very good, Spirit!" Master Nomi smiled. "In order to get it, in order for your goal to arrive in your life by itself, you must first let go—in nature, nothing is forced. All things occur and manifest themselves from their own 'seed potentials.' There is a natural potential in everything, in each of us, which grows of itself. Sometimes we only need to cultivate it for our seed potential to realize itself. There must be no *Self* behind this action; there must be no '*me*,' no 'I' which forces the action for its own sake. This is what we call *unconditioned* effort, which is very different from a *conditioned* effort that may have its roots in your past experience, as when your parents instructed you—thinking they were doing the right thing—to push yourself to get results for the sake of succeeding. And what is succeeding? Is it not personal happiness and contentment that you have each come here to find? Is it not wanting to know that you have fulfilled your own potential, like a tiger catching its prey? There is no Self directing the effort of the tiger. It is an action based upon *unconditioned effort* or *non-action,* which is the natural seed potential of the tiger. It is *No Mind*."

"We all have natural abilities and talents," Master Nomi continued. "We need only to *not try* for these inner potentialities to manifest themselves, just as a seed needs no effort or force to grow into a tree, since the tree, potentially, is in the seed. Therefore, each of us has our own *tree* in our birth-seed. And with natural, unconditioned effort, we allow it to spring forth and grow. Sometimes it is difficult to see the tree in the seed."

This reminded Mindful of something he once heard a coach tell a competitor who was training for a sporting event: "Try to just be in the moment and not think about the goal or the result. Don't block the effort by trying too hard and overcompensating."

"That's right," Spirit agreed. "I think when we *try* too hard, even to find God, all we find is Scripture and not the experience. And that's like looking into the cloudy water, isn't it? I once heard a priest give a sermon that emphasized *letting go* in order to experience God directly. It really resonated with me."

Master Nomi turned to Spirit and said, "Yes, we find the cloudy water and lose sight of the bottom of the pond. These ancient paradoxes come from truths that have been with humanity for thousands of years—since we first discovered what the ancient masters called the *self-nature,* or what you might call *spiritual awareness.* We all share the same seed potential of enlightenment, it is in our genes. We all seek the *something more.* These paradoxes guide us in developing our full potential. You will learn that application of this basic idea of *not trying* will allow your full seed potential to sprout and grow. Know your potential, and let it manifest of its own accord without thinking what you *should* do, or how you *should* have performed, or thinking what everyone else says you *should* do."

"I think I get it now," Iill said. "My potential was to succeed as a businessman. But even when I became successful, I still wasn't fulfilled completely. I pushed myself with great effort to prove something to myself and others, but the only result was more stress, sometimes to the point of getting physically sick. I also got into some negative habits to handle the pressure. So I understand what you're saying. What I really needed to do was eliminate all the *shoulds* and expectations that I and others forced upon me. Maybe all those times I wasted being sick or stressed out could have been avoided."

"Pressure itself is not bad," said Master Nomi, as he moved to the second scroll. "For even as water flows between rocks in a stream, it flows with more force due to the natural pressure created by the rocks. The water reacts naturally to the obstacles in its path. The stream does not need a pump to push the water downstream, and all the water will eventually end up in the same place. Recognize that your actions and reactions to the world around you create a natural flow and force. When encountering the rocks in your stream of life, the pressure will increase as it does in the stream, but know that this is natural. Don't fight it by *trying* to stop it. Simply move with it until there is calm water, and then you will act with greater efficiency. All you need to do is remove your conditioned artificial idea of having to *try* to "pump the water." The 'I' produces the *artificial pump* to force the water to where it would have gone naturally if left alone, just as a seed will become a tree even when you pay no attention to it."

"Exactly," Mindful chimed in. "When I perform by just letting go and losing myself in the moment, I actually perform better. That's what the *zone* and peak performance are all about, aye!"

Chapter 5:
Paradox Two

Master Nomi directed the three travelers to focus on the Second Paradox:

ACT. REACT.
BUT ALWAYS IN PLAY.

"When you completely forget about *trying*," he said, "you return to the natural wonder of play that you experienced as a child. You forget this as you become an adult and lose your spontaneity. It is easy to not see this change taking place. As your ego was developing and you became competitive, you began to identify with your self-image, your team, your school, your city. Each time you identified with something, you lost the play in what you did. Thus, you *missed the play in the game*. Instead, you need to allow yourselves to simply *play for the sake of playing* and nothing else—no goal, just the process."

"You're absolutely right, mate," Mindful said. "When I play just for the sake of playing, it's a lot more fun, and I really enjoy the game. Usually, though, my mates and I stress out about who will win. We worry about sponsors, money, and fame, and in the process we lose sight of the purpose of the game. That purpose is to play because we want to, and to have a good time. Aye, I can apply that Paradox to my life."

Iill readily identified with what Mindful was saying. "Yes, it's true," he agreed. "I've definitely lost the play in my work. People in business are so serious and concerned with outcomes, they miss out on the fun and excitement of the entire process. I've been like that for years—stressed out, full of anxiety, worried, and somehow always feeling like I have to keep catching up. The stress of trying so hard to achieve outcomes is unhealthy and, all too often, enemies are made along the path to monetary success. We all need to pay more attention to finding the *play* in what we do." I now realize that there is a more productive way—and most important, a healthier way."

"Yes," Master Nomi concurred. "This is what the ancient masters called *serving the task*. It is the selfless act of just *doing* and not thinking about results. This is doing for the sake of doing, as in Original Play."

"Original play?" Iill asked.

Master Nomi explained. "It's the natural action of the universe from which all life and non-life is manifested, as when the rays of the Sun travel millions of miles through space to give life to a flower. Original Play is everything that happens unintentionally in nature: seeds grow, suns explode, planets evolve, water flows. The universe doesn't have intention or expectations. The universe simply *selflessly acts* and *everything is done.*"

Iill thought for a moment. "So it is a playful ritual of natural order," he said, "unlike the rituals we use in society that many times are so unnatural and have false intentions."

Spirit, too, was eager to share her thoughts. "That's exactly one of the things wrong with religion today," she said. "People are so concerned about ritual, so used to standing on ceremony; they forget there's supposed to be a *direct* spiritual experience in their belief. They forget the play in their faith and get all involved in the 'have-to's' rather than the process. I do it myself. I focus on Scripture and ceremony instead of getting into the direct experience. No question, that is why I'm looking for my Zen. It's as you said, Master Nomi, *the more you look, the farther you move away from it*."

The Master was quite pleased with Spirit's assessment. "You each have great potential to use the Ten Paradoxes and the Secrets of No Mind," he said. "You realize their importance. The entire universe works on the concept of play, as there is no *selfish* intention in any aspect of nature, only *selfless* action. It is exactly like children playing. They are sometimes so engrossed in the play that they become *selfless;* there is only the game for them and nothing else. This is the true play of No Mind. When we no longer choose sides in the game, we play effortlessly and thus our perform-ance increases. We lose the tight competitive mind-body hold that can keep us from our full potential. We also lose the 'self' and its socially imposed expectations."

"That's for sure, losing the self in true play would be great," Spirit said. "And how easy it is to get blocked by our persistent expectations and our *shoulds!*"

"Correct," said Master Nomi. "We are blocked, which is not natural; therefore, we fail to achieve our peak performance. Play is the acting and reacting that we do every day without the ego, without the Self. When we truly play, we are in the *Now;* we are not focused on future worries or past regrets or past guilt. We act because it is our natural tendency to act, just as a hawk can fly in circles for a long time, fully enjoying the wind without flapping its wings. The hawk plays in the air currents and simply *becomes* the wind by fulfilling its natural seed potential. In that moment, the hawk and the wind are one and the same. We all have our natural seed potentials, and through play we reflect them in the world."

"When I get back to my office," said Iill, "I will tell my staff that we need to be at play and not be so serious. They'll look at me like I'm crazy and wonder what really happened on my trip," he laughed. "Most people see play as games and having fun, and work as serious and stressful. Very few enjoy both at the same time, which is really what you are saying we need to be doing."

Master Nomi nodded in agreement. "Many people have not experienced that reality of nature," he said. "It is only our intentions and expectations which make work *work* and not play. When at work, we would rather be doing something else; we become consumed with the goal, or work becomes boring through repetition. But all we need to do is focus on the work in the moment and learn to discover the play. We need to work without the conditioned effort and any ego-intention so it can become play. When, like children, we are able to lose ourselves in the play and become the game, only then do we learn to perform at our optimum best. We simply *lose ourselves* in the work and *serve the task*."

Once again, Mindful was reminded of what his coach had advised: 'Lose yourself in the action of the game. Just play without trying to prove anything. Then you will be in the *zone,* and be at your best.' "Good stuff, all right," Mindful had to admit.

Then Master Nomi invited them to walk outside to the lanai, which overlooked a beautiful Zen garden with Japanese stone lanterns, meditation statues, stone ornaments, and a pagoda. The sun was setting, its final glimmer shining through the tall bamboo, casting its rays across the garden. The sound of a waterfall played over the silence. He turned to the three travelers. "You are probably thirsty and hungry after your journey. Sit here on the cushions around the table, and I will return with tea."

Chapter 6: **Paradox Three**

Master Nomi soon returned, carrying a tray with a small tea bowl, a water kettle, a whisk, a scoop, a tea container and Okashi dumplings made of kneaded, salted ground soybeans filled with persimmon and nuts. "This sweet bun, called Chinese fruit," he explained, "is served well with tea." He placed the tray on the table and said, "Try to allow your mind to be without thoughts of anything else except watching the preparation of the tea and drinking of the tea. Try to feel every sensation, hear every sound, taste without comparing, smell the aromas, including the incense and flowers, and be mindful of everything around you. When you become aware of these things, you will lose yourself in your actions. The larger water kettle, called *mizusashi,* represents the Sun and is *Yang;* the small tea bowl, called *chawan,* represents the Moon and is *Yin.* These are the two forces of nature which balance everything. They are not opposites, but only two aspects of the essence of nature."

"You will learn to discover pure awareness, which your mind now consumes," he continued. "When your awareness is free of mind, we call this *No Mind.* Awareness is as much an aspect of the body and the mind as it an aspect of the universe. We learn this by becoming mindful of our actions. We can practice it in everything we do. So let us now perform the tea ceremony."

Master Nomi lifted the tea scoop and container and carefully placed twelve tea scoops into the tea bowl. He then ladled hot water from the kettle into the tea bowl, using the whisk to mix the tea. He added a little more water and whisked some more. Then he passed the bowl to Spirit, rotating it as he gave it to her. She took the bowl with two hands and nodded in thanks. "Admire the bowl," he began. "Drink. Feel the taste sensation of the tea in your mouth, then in your throat. Wipe the rim of the bowl, and pass it to Mindful. Be aware of every sensation and thought, and just let them pass. Watch the thoughts without giving them any more energy. In this way, your mind opens to perceive reality directly."

The bowl was returned to Master Nomi after Iill had taken the last drink, and then Mindful said, "My father taught me to meditate many years ago. This is like a meditation."

Iill, in particular, paid careful attention to everything that was going on. "I have never drunk tea like this before," he admitted. "When I eat, I'm always doing or thinking about five different things at the same time. Either that, or I talk while I'm eating, and I never really get to be aware of the true enjoyment of the food. So this is a very 'thoughtless' experience," Iill smiled.

"Exactly," Master Nomi acknowledged. "We need to have No Mind to experience the full potential of our senses and experience reality with a clearer, direct perception. Through the tea cere-mony, we develop No Mind using the practice of *Clear Attention,* or what other masters have called 'mindfulness.' When we are *mindful* of everything we are experiencing in the present moment, we separate our awareness from our thoughts. During this mindfulness, we realize thoughts and awareness can be separated, which allows us to 'see and feel' more clearly. On the other hand, when we experience *mindlessness,* our thoughts and awareness have merged, clouding the water, in effect, so that we are never fully clear and aware. Without realizing it, we end up acting like automatons; we are on autopilot.

"You see, the harder we try thinking about where our Zen is, the more we fall into the mindless trap and become stuck. Therefore, we must seek to understand through the act of *not* thinking, or No Mind. Now you have learned the Third Paradox:

SEEK MIND WITH NO THOUGHT.

Mindful, Iill and Spirit were fascinated. "We can never experience No Mind with mind," Master Nomi continued. "Therefore, when we have *no thought,* we see the mind for what it really is: a mechanism of memory, categories, associations, emotions, and intellect, all of which are byproducts of the brain's mapping structure and chemistry.

It's a mental web in which our awareness is trapped." He paused to emphasize what he wanted them to remember. "When mind consumes awareness, we have mindlessness. When awareness consumes mind, we have mindfulness."

"So our mind blocks our pure awareness?" Spirit asked, clearly trying to absorb what she had heard. "Are you saying that the more concerned we are with what we've learned and what we know, the harder it is to see what's really there? If I understand this correctly, the mind traps itself, but when we step out of this trap we see the whole reality. Is that right?"

"Yes, exactly," said Master Nomi, delighted at Spirit's perception and insight. "You remove the duality of yourself from the knowing. Instead of saying 'I know that,' there is *just the knowing*. The more you study mind, the farther away you move from your true nature. It is like attempting to view the back of your head with your eyes. When searching for your Zen, the more you seek, the more you will *not* find it. Only when you have *no thought* will you then understand mind."

"I don't really understand that yet," said Iill. "I was always taught 'Look and ye shall find it.'"

"Amen!" Spirit said with a smile.

Chapter 7:
Paradox Four

Master Nomi gave them both a pointed stare, saying, "Think about *Who* is looking. It is exactly the premise of the Who that we shall discuss and which keeps you from finding what you seek. When we look to the beginning of a thought, or the mind before the thought began, we can simply ask, '*Who* is thinking?' This is what the ancient masters called the *hua-t'ou* or, literally, the head of the thought. When you realize that the Who is an illusion of the mind, then you will know where your Zen is."

"I was there once, during a game," Mindful interjected. "It was a peak experience. I was in the 'zone.' For those few brief moments, there was no *Who* and there was no *Me*. Honestly, mate, there was only the playing of the game, as if the bleemin' game was being played right through my mind and body. It was an experience I've had a hard time putting into words."

"In that moment, Mindful, you knew where your Zen was," said Master Nomi, stepping down from the lanai. "The *Who* we speak of cannot exist in the present moment. There is only pure awareness. There is only No Mind. This is what is called *looking into the emptiness*. And this is the basis of the Fourth Paradox."

He then moved into the pebble garden, walked over to the pond, and looked down at the ripples where the waterfall was trickling into the pond. "Who makes the ripples on the water?"

"No one," said Iill. "The water falling into the pond makes the ripples. There is no *Who*. It is just natural."

"That's right," Mindful added, smiling at Spirit. "It's just gravity and the water hitting the water. Don't have to be a genius for that one, aye?"

"So there is no *intention* of the water falling into the pond to make the ripples. It is only a natural action and reaction," Master Nomi concluded. He then bent down, picked up a pebble and threw it into the pond, causing ripples across its surface. A duck that was floating close to where the stone landed was startled and flew into the air. "*Now* is there a 'Who' behind those ripples in the water? And was there intention in the action?"

"You made the ripples by throwing the pebble," Spirit replied. "And, yes, it was your intention to throw the pebble, and *you* caused the ripples to happen and make the duck fly away. So the ripples spreading across the water were the pond's reaction to your intentional action."

"And what if there *were* no intention?" Master Nomi asked. "Would the action have been natural like the waterfall striking the pond's surface?"

Iill struggled for an answer. "How can you throw the pebble without intention?" he asked. "Don't you need to have an intention to throw it, basically saying to yourself, 'I will now throw the pebble at the water'? On the other hand, the waterfall hitting the pond and causing ripples is an action of nature."

"Yes, of course, it is natural," Master Nomi answered. "But so is the lizard snatching the fly from a leaf with its tongue. It has no intention based on its Self or ego or Who, and that is where intention starts. The lizard is acting in accord with its natural potential, as is the hawk gliding on the currents of the wind. There is no ego-based intention here. The lizard and the hawk have one thing in common: there is no Who behind their actions. If that is so, can I not throw the pebble into the pond *without intention* if I take the Who out of the action? When action flows through mind and body without the ego's intention, then throwing the pebble is as natural as the hawk gliding or the swift tongue of the lizard."

After presenting this quandary, Master Nomi moved around to a large stepped boulder protruding from the other side of the pond. He walked up the natural rock stairway and stood atop the boulder, lifting his hands into the air, silhouetted by the setting sun behind him. "This," he said, "is the principle of karma and the Fourth Paradox:

WITH THOUGHT, INTENTION.
WITH INTENTION, KARMA.

"Be clear about this," he cautioned. "Karma is not based on action and reaction, as many people believe. It is governed by intention and action guided by a Who. Karma does not exist in nature. When a tree falls in the forest, when a star explodes in the heavens, there is no Who behind the action. Therefore, there is no karma. Karma is a human condition like evil. Evil does not exist anywhere in nature except in the human world. When we remove the Who from our actions, we are free of karma. It is said that those who are enlightened no longer experience karma in their lives. Having the experience of enlightenment is one thing, but living by *enlightened action* is another."

As though thinking out loud, Spirit spoke deliberately, measuring her words. "So it is the *Who* that is preventing me from discovering God-consciousness or enlightenment," she began. "If I 'see through' the Who, I can get rid of karma and reach God-consciousness. Is this what you're saying?"

Before Master Nomi could reply, she continued: "In the *Kabbalah,* the ancient book of Hebrew mysticism, it is written: 'Who is a hero? The one who controls his passion.' I interpret this as telling us that when we control the desires of our Self or the Who, we discover selflessness and eventually spiritual growth. Sometimes by *not* acting, we are truly the hero of our self."

"Even control is intention," Master Nomi noted. "When your seeds of intention are gone, you will be free of cause and effect. As long as you see the positive and negative effects, you are still bound by karma. When you are beyond the opposites, beyond desire and control, then you will know where your Zen is. It is thought that brings intentions. It is thought that limits performance and potential. And it is intention that brings with it karma."

Chapter 8:
Paradox Five

The Master walked over to a small hut that stood behind the pond. It was starting to grow dark, so he lit some small kerosene lanterns. He excused himself and stepped inside the hut. A few moments later, he emerged wearing an evil mask with large teeth, red beady eyes, and horns that protruded from each side. He stood in the shadows of the flickering lantern. Mindful, Iill and Spirit were startled by his appearance, their apprehension obvious as they exchanged wary glances. "Wait a minute," whispered

Spirit. "This is obviously another one of Master Nomi's demonstrations. Let's play along."

"Are you going to be performing an act, Master Nomi?" Iill asked with a tentative smile and began to applaud the Master's new costume. Mindful and Spirit cheerfully joined in.

"All right, mate," Mindful laughed. "Looks like we're going to have a bit of fun this evening."

"I could tell that your initial reaction was fear," said Master Nomi, "until you realized there was nothing to fear. Throughout the day, our mind matches things we see and sorts them into our learned categories. By doing this, our mind creates representations of reality, which limits its full *natural* potential to perform without prejudice. The mind is inhibited by its own inherent neural trap from perceiving the actuality of reality.

"The mask represents fear because we have *learned* that such an evil mask could represent something harmful. When you discovered that no harm was meant, your thinking mind corrected its perception."

Master Nomi removed the mask and walked to the lanai, where he lit additional lanterns that were hanging from posts. "Our minds do this habitually hundreds of times a day," he continued. "and so we prejudice, categorize, and identify everything around us. This compromises our ability to see things as they *really* are, to see them more clearly and directly."

Iill nodded in agreement. "I understand this only too well," he said. "It's true. We make decisions all the time based on thinking that what we've learned will be right for a given situation. Although these may not be the best decisions, we make them because we're comfortable with them. They fit into our mind box, and we often block ourselves from *seeing* a better solution. I have done this many times in my life. I find myself completely regulated by convention, ego satisfaction, rules, and what I *should* do. I'm tired of it, and it sure doesn't bring me the happiness I seek. In fact, I know I don't work at my peak potential because of it, which is one of the reasons I am here."

"Absolutely," Spirit agreed, "especially in the religious world, where everything has to be a certain way because it was 'so written.' All the religious education in the world, all the 'must-do's' and 'should-haves,' do not give us the direct experience of God. These things only give us education and understanding *without experience.*"

"Right," Mindful chimed in. "I remember play-ing many games where I was trying to please my father; I felt the pressure to *please,* and I couldn't really perform the right way. As much as I wanted to, I couldn't be at my best. It's like I was pre-programmed to please and do what I was *supposed* to do. All those *shoulds* again, mate ... not good!"

"Yes, it is a paradox," Master Nomi continued. "When we over-think, it often hurts our perform-ance. So in order to perform better, we need to learn to *un-think*. We need to allow mind and body to perform through No Mind. In this way, we *un-condition* ourselves so we can perform unconditionally, fulfilling our natural potential. When we do this, we allow the mind and body to *naturally* do what each of us has the natural potential to do. We then can experience peak performance."

Master Nomi finished lighting the lanterns as the sky reflected the last half-hour of daylight. In the distance, the sunset colored the horizon orange and then pink. He turned to face Mindful, Iill, and Spirit as they gathered closer to him. "When you become lost in your thought patterns, you hinder your performance," the Master told them. "When you intuitively grasp the solution to a problem, without over-thinking and over-analyzing it, your solutions are more likely to be superior. Remember that your *true intuitions* are outside the mind box of learned categorizations and intellectual patterns."

"So when we think less," Iill suggested excitedly, "we perform better and our solutions to problems are more intuitive? That is certainly what I need in my business—better performance and more intuitive decisions, yes, sir."

"Aye," said Mindful. "When I over-think my moves in a game, I don't do very well either. I do best when I trust myself to *just play.* Too much thinking can cripple someone's performance."

Master Nomi again offered a revelation. "This is the Fifth Paradox," he said.

PERFORM. DO.
BUT NEVER THINK.

"In this way, we *un-condition* our performance, and that makes all the difference. We lose ourselves in the part much like actors on the stage of life. We un-condition the *shoulds* and *must-do's,* so that what remains is just *pure action.* Remember, we need only remove the mask of ourselves. We need to see through the Who of our actions … to see the beginning of the thought: the *hua t'ou.*"

心を鏡とすれば全てが現われる

Chapter 9:
Paradox Six

Master Nomi began to walk back to the pond and signaled the others to join him. He stood at the water's edge, gazing into it. The three followed the Master's lead and looked down at the pond. The colorful twilight clouds were reflected on its still surface, producing a kaleidoscope of light. The bamboo that stood on the opposite edge of the pond swayed slightly in the breeze, its stalks reflected as dark silhouettes on the water's surface. Suddenly, a bird flew overhead, and they all watched its reflection moving across the twilight-colored water.

"The water reflects whatever stands before it, and it does so without discrimination," said Master Nomi. "It acts as a pure mirror. There was *no intention* of the pond to reflect the bird, and the bird had *no intention* of being reflected in the pond. Yet both were revealed. As I mentioned before, even when there is no intention, pure actions are still naturally performed. The pond is like a movie screen displaying what is projected upon it, and makes no choice."

"Which brings us," said the Master, "to the Sixth Paradox:

WHEN MIND IS A MIRROR, EVERYTHING IS REVEALED.

"In the study of No Mind, we become mindful of everything around us and in us, yet we do not use the mind to analyze the objects themselves. They are simply reflected across the mind's screen of awareness. In this way, we merely observe objectively."

"What does it mean that everything is revealed?" Spirit asked.

"When we are truly reflecting, as the pond does, and we have no intention, the Self and Non-Self—what is the Who and what is *not* the Who—

are revealed," the Master replied. "We pierce the mind's veil of discriminations. When this happens, we see reality directly, and we then experience No Mind—our true spiritual awareness that links us to all of nature, or the *Tao*."

"So we can experience God directly?" Spirit asked enthusiastically. "Is this what the ancient mystics called God-consciousness? It reminds me of something I learned in the *Kabbalah*: 'The Breath becomes a stone; the stone, a plant; the plant, an animal; the animal, a man; the man, a spirit; and the spirit, a god."

"Yes," said Master Nomi gently. "Whatever your belief, you can experience the essence of that belief by separating awareness from the Who. Thus, you eliminate the mind as a discriminator in what you perceive, allowing you to see more clearly than ever before. This is how we gain the insight of our innate nature, our pure Self, devoid of ego. And at this point, there is a perceptual shift that needs to be *experienced* and not just intellectually understood. It is the first level of enlightenment from which there is no return, and although nothing has changed, nothing will ever be the same again."

"Wow, that sounds heavy, mate," Mindful said. "Are you saying we can see into the nature of reality? Into the nature of our true Self? I learned to meditate as a kid. We used to focus on one thing and on our breathing. It was a little different than becoming a mirror, but I get it."

After gazing into the pond for a few moments, the Master turned and walked back toward the lanai. "Let's go inside," he said. "It's getting dark. I will briefly demonstrate a technique for you that can be applied in your daily lives in many ways."

"You know, I can see how valuable it would be to be able to mirror your perceptions, even in a difficult business meeting," Iill said. "By becoming an observer of my own inner reactions and being able to *mirror* what is going on in a meeting, I'd be able to see clearly what is 'really' happening. Instead of trying to pigeonhole everything into what I think 'should' happen, I'd have better control and the ability to unemotionally negotiate, as well as come up with more creative solutions outside my mind-box."

"Exactly," the Master replied. "When you mirror the other person's actions, whether in sports, a business partner, or even your lover, your mind's filter is removed, and you perceive from a more intuitive source. This is known as *direct perception*. This is the ancient secret of the Samurai warrior. To the extent that he is experiencing No Mind, the sword finds nowhere to strike him."

Iill wondered how this could be. "Are you saying the sword cannot find him?" he asked.

"It is written in the *Tao*," replied Master Nomi. "In battle, weapons cannot touch him. The buffalo's horn finds nowhere to jab. The tiger's claw, no place to grip. Why is this so? Because in him there is no place for death to enter. When you *know* where your Zen is, then you will understand what this means."

The Master went through the lanai and into the doorway. One by one, the windows were illuminated as he lit a series of candles; then he moved on to lighting the lanterns in the main hall, where he had first encountered the three travelers. As the group followed along, they again observed the Ten Paradoxes hanging on the walls. Master Nomi walked past the table where the ancient stone rested in its glass case, then through a beautiful hand-carved doorway into the next room.

There were four floor cushions arranged in a square around a large statue in the center. The statue was an intricately carved tall stone depicting four seated Zen monks, each facing one of the four cardinal points. The monks were in meditation positions: one hand outstretched, palm forward; the other resting, palm side up, in their laps. Each hand that rested on a lap held a candle, which Master Nomi proceeded to light. He then motioned to the three to join him as they all sat down on the cushions, each facing a different side of the stone statue.

"The gesture of the outstretched left hand means *do not fear,*" the Master explained. "And the candles facing all four cardinal points means that you draw light or energy from all around you, not from any one point. The right hand on the lap symbolizes the union of method and skill to overcome the mind by emptying your awareness of all thoughts. When practicing this No Mind technique, your perception eventually is holistically changed so that you no longer see only what is before you, but all around you, as well. This is developing the insight of spiritual awareness, or No Mind."

"Therefore," he continued, "we begin learning how to reflect like the pond by practicing the technique of No Mind. The pond has no intention to reflect anything; it is merely the intrinsic nature of the water to be able to reflect. The water does not need to learn anything in order to reflect what is projected upon it. In the same way, the awareness does not need to learn anything to become a mirror; it is innately and naturally a mirror. Yet, our minds have the ability to consume, or absorb, awareness. Every time we do this, we become mindless; we act on autopilot. By contrast, when we detach the awareness from mind, we become mindful instead of mindless, and therefore we clear the mind in order to reflect clearly. Remember, when a cloudy film covers the surface of the water, it can no longer reflect purely what is before it. This technique allows our minds to become purified of the cloudy film of the ego, or the Who, so we can reflect like a mirror. Then, we achieve pure awareness."

"So what you're saying," Spirit offered, making herself comfortable on the cushion, "is that all of our conditioning, learning, habits, emotions, and thoughts cloud our ability to see what is really there. And that in order to know where our Zen is, we need to remove the cloudy film of our mind to see with pure eyes."

Iill began to tally his own conclusions. "It's a matter of reflecting what is really in front of us without trying to describe it or pigeonhole it, so to speak," he said. "You're saying that this allows us to understand reality from a different perspective. Then our decisions are made with a clearer, less conditioned mind—one that is much more effective."

"Yes," Master Nomi said, "you are beginning to understand part of the equation. You will still need to practice the technique in order to clear the cloudy film of mind away and *untrain* the categorizations of mind. This is similar to what a well-known Western psychologist called de-automatization."

He then grabbed a bamboo stick which was leaning against the wall, walked around the three students, and instructed them to sit in a comfortable position. "Make sure your spine is erect," he said. "Close your eyes and then slightly open them so you can barely see the candle before you; this will keep you focused on the present and slow the natural tendency to fall asleep. Breathe from your stomach into your lungs. Draw the energy of the candle into your stomach by breathing into it, expanding it, and lowering your diaphragm. Now, fill the upper lungs with air and expand the chest. This is the cycle of breathing in one slow, continuous movement. You will develop a rhythm by breathing in half as long as you exhale. For every four counts you inhale, you breathe out eight counts. If you become sleepy or begin to slouch, I will tap you on your shoulder with this stick to bring your focus back to the present. Focus on your breathing, and let your awareness become clear of thoughts and mind objects. That is all. Let us begin."

The three began their practice of the technique. After a time, Iill started to slouch, his head lowering as if he were falling asleep. Master Nomi went behind him and tapped him firmly on the shoulders with the bamboo stick.

"Ow!" Iill exclaimed, quickly regaining his posture and focus. Mindful and Spirit, wanting to avoid the bamboo stick, similarly adjusted their postures.

The Master, meanwhile, encircled them and spoke softly. "When you become aware of mind objects such as thoughts, ideas, and feelings, including your bodily sensations," he said, "allow them to simply float through your awareness without giving them any more energy. Let them pass over the screen of awareness. The more you acknowledge them and analyze them, the more they will consume your awareness. Your awareness is like a mirror, and you can reflect mind objects just as the water in the pond reflected the passing bird and the sky above. Remember, it is an intrinsic aspect of clear water to reflect, just as it is an intrinsic aspect of clear awareness to reflect. Your purpose is to clear the awareness from the cloudy film of mind objects. In this way, the cloudy water becomes clear and the glimmer of the stone is seen."

As the evening wore on, Mindful, Iill and Spirit couldn't keep from shifting and slouching. Master Nomi had to firmly tap each of them on the shoulders at least three times. Finally, he clapped his hands twice and said, "Let us continue our dialogue."

"I think my legs are numb," Iill admitted. "I need to get up and stretch."

"Yup," Mindful added, "I need some stretching all right."

At this point, they all arose, stretched, and moved about.

"I loved that!" Spirit enthused. "I was really beginning to feel connected and at peace. I was letting everything go and filling my awareness with pure God-energy. It was quite inspiring."

"Well," Iill said, "I don't know about reflecting God, but I was reflecting that candle in my mind. In fact, at one point there was just the candle and the awareness of the candle. It was great! I feel so refreshed."

Meanwhile, Mindful continued to sit in silence while Master Nomi explained:

"The soreness of legs and feet will disappear with practice. But the important thing to remember is this: *You need to learn to do this anywhere—* while washing dishes, riding on the subway, or walking in the park. You must become aware of your surroundings, your inner body feelings, and your mind contents throughout the day by practicing this technique. By doing so, you will rediscover the natural ability of awareness to simply reflect, just as clear water does. This is an innate ability. When we were infants, it was natural, but we lost the ability as the 'ego' developed."

"So," Mindful summarized, "we are basically detoxifying the mind of its mind objects—sort of purifying our awareness so we can gain insight into experiencing where our Zen is? Is that about right, Master Nomi?"

"That is about right, yes," Master Nomi laughed. "We cleanse the awareness from the mind. We purify our perceptions and objectively see the discriminations we make of everything. We are again removing the mask or, even better, removing the colored lens through which we otherwise see. In this way, we remove the cloudy film from our perceptions, so we do not feel the need to identify and categorize everything. Being mindful and not mindless allows us to function in a much more effective way."

考えれば生まれず、考えなければ生れ出る

Chapter 10:
Paradox Seven

The Master walked back through the doorway to where the Ten Paradoxes were displayed. The others followed. "Let us move on to the Seventh Paradox," he said. "I believe this will now be much easier for you to understand. It is:

WITH THOUGHT,
NO FLOW.
WITHOUT THOUGHT,
FLOW.

"That reminds me of the stream of water and the boulders, which seems like a good metaphor," Spirit observed.

"Yes, good!" Master Nomi replied. "When there is resistance, as the boulder in the stream, the water is forced to move faster and with stronger intensity in order to get around it. Yet, no matter, it still flows around it. The greater the resistance, as with a large boulder as opposed to a smaller one, the greater the speed and intensity. Thoughts, like boulders in the stream, cause the mind to lose the flow, become more resistant, and move with greater intensity."

The Master looked at each of them, from one to the next to the next, and added, "Think about when you were fearful of something. At first, you experienced a slight nervousness. Then, when your mind produced additional thoughts of the possibility of an impending danger, your nervousness became anxiety. If you really lost control of your thoughts, the anxiety turned to panic. And all of this transpired, not because of the reality of the situation, but only because of your run-away thoughts. Thoughts can allow a simple fear to grow into terror. The more productive, efficient, and in control you are, the *less* you think. It is a paradox."

"It seems to me, then," Spirit noted, "that too many religious thoughts also block the flow of experiencing God directly. It makes sense, doesn't it?" she asked. "The more boulders in the stream, the more we focus on the boulders—or the thoughts, and the less we focus on the flow of the stream—or the present moment … which, from what you said, Master Nomi, is the only way we ever really know where our Zen is."

The master nodded in agreement. "Thoughts disrupt the flow of our true potential. Therefore, when we are without thoughts, we practice being in the pure flow of our self-nature. Instead of being consumed by the mind's thoughts, we practice No Mind, or no-thought. As long as we are trapped in our thoughts, we get caught up in the rapids and become mindless instead of mindful."

"One time, when I got hurt playing on the field during a rugby match," Mindful recalled, "I thought something was seriously wrong because I couldn't move my legs. The fear turned to panic. My blood pressure shot up and I was like a ravin' lunatic. They had to sedate me just to calm me down. I really lost control of my thoughts and made it a lot worse than it was. It was a temporary paralysis caused by the ball hitting me in my back. Fortunately, I was fine within the hour. But at first I really lost control because I let my thoughts get the best of me."

Iill concurred, saying, "People make bad decisions based on fear. It seems to me that thoughts based on other strong emotions, like greed, jealousy, resentment, hate, prejudice, and so on, can run equally wild. Those types of negative thoughts can escalate quickly and get out of control in no time. It's the way a stock market decline gets accelerated by negative fears: before you know it, the ensuing panic sends the index plummeting, and then—crash!"

Iill wondered, "How many problems, both individual and global, would be prevented if people could expand their awareness beyond these basic mind mechanisms and learn to follow the flow or even slow down between the rapids to see the authenticity of their lives?"

"Thought is a natural function of mind," the Master said. "When thoughts are based on fears, expectations, and discrimination, they hinder us more than they help us. Those thoughts also influence our behavior and perception of the world. During my own research over the past two and a half decades, I found that many psychologists started discovering that thoughts may impede the proper functioning of decision-making when the mind tries to over-think and over-analyze solutions to problems. And our creativity and intuitions are blocked. We need to be able to recognize our intuitions and learn to trust them instead."

Master Nomi then reached for the lantern near the door and walked outside, signaling the others to follow. The four moved across the lanai into the rock garden, guided by the flickering lantern along the small gravel path.

"When the mind is balanced," Master Nomi explained, "it is like the stream flowing along its natural course and doing what is intrinsic to its nature. When the mind is disrupted with emotions, its flow becomes pressured like the water flowing around the boulders in the stream. If mind is likened to water, then as the emotions become more intense, it will become steam—unfocused and ungrounded. On the other hand, when the mind is frozen on the same thoughts, as when we are unhappy or depressed, then it is like ice or slush and loses its natural flow."

"What I think you're saying, Master Nomi, is that we don't want to get stuck on a thought, or have too many thoughts—as is the case when our mind races," Iill said as he followed the Master down the path. "But if our thoughts are a natural product of the mind, as you say they are, then we need to learn how to simply allow our actions to flow without manipulating or over-thinking them. We use thoughts as a tool, right? And not as a 'read-out on reality.' I take it, then, the main point is that we *do not* have to *act* on our thoughts."

"This is true," Master Nomi agreed. "But only when you take the Who out of the thought. When our thoughts are of the present moment, we are more like the water flowing in the stream and flowing around the boulders. In the present moment, there is no Who. *When you walk, think of walking only, and not about anything else.* Remember, when walking, just walk. Thoughts of the Who ... of the 'I'... will only slow you down, slow the flow, and you won't perform as well. And if you do not remove the Who from the action, you could easily get stuck."

Master Nomi looked around, as if trying to find something, and added, "Remember, our thoughts are sticky like a spider's web."

The Master searched among the trees, shining the lantern everywhere, and finally walked over to an old chest that was resting on the ground against a pine tree. "Ah, it is here," he said, setting down the lantern. He opened the chest and gazed inside. He then reached in, moved things around with his hand, pulled out a large flashlight, put it in his robe pocket and said, "Let's continue." As they walked farther down the path through the pines, the fog began rolling in, obscuring the way ahead. The flame of the lantern reflected through the fog, casting an eerie glow.

Mindful, walking directly behind the Master, asked, "So, Master Nomi, if you just focus on the present moment of the activity, you'll be in the flow, right?" He paused, adding, "Aye, just don't let the thoughts keep consuming your awareness. I get it now!"

Spirit added, "And let go of the 'I'—the *Who*, as Master Nomi calls it. We need to let go of the *thoughts* of ourselves and trust our mind and body to do what they *know* how to do. *That's* how we know where our Zen is. Perhaps that is what Jesus meant when he said, 'The Kingdom of God is within you.' By losing the Who, we see the Kingdom of God. We can only see God after the Who is overcome." Spirit peered down to make sure she could see the path in front of her.

The Master stopped walking, removed the flashlight from his pocket and shined the beam of light between two pine trees, revealing a massive spider web sparkling with dew. A large spider rested motionless in the middle of the web, droplets of water glistening on its back. Suddenly, a beautiful gray and brown moth, attracted to the light, flew across the beam, landed in the web, and became stuck. The moth fluttered, attempting to escape, but remained trapped.

"I feel bad for that moth," Spirit said. "It's lost its freedom to fly through the night. Its life has ended."

"Yet," Master Nomi began, "is it not the spider that has always been stuck in the web and has never known the freedom that the moth knows? Throughout the spider's life, it has only known the confines of the web. The moth, however, has been able to fly freely wherever the wind has taken it."

"But the spider needs the web in order to survive," Iill said as he watched the struggling moth. "Otherwise it wouldn't be able to catch its food. So I guess it's stuck in the web because it needs the web, and knows no other life except for the web. I think many people are like the spider. They are stuck in their own webs."

"Very good!" Master Nomi said, pleased with Iill's insight. "Indeed, our minds create a mental web based on our ego, our self-image, or the Who. It is the brain's natural mechanism to create these webs by categorizing and associating everything that comes before it. We become attached to desires, expectations, hopes, thoughts, beliefs, needs, motivations—all the things we think we need to make us complete and whole. Our ego divides us into parts, preventing us from being whole. We don't realize that we are trapped by this mental web until we attempt to escape it. Then, like the moth, we realize the struggle to free ourselves may be impossible—yet it is doable. Of course, this depends on the extent to which we are stuck and how many points of our web we are stuck to."

"What do you mean by *whole*?" asked Mindful. "Aren't we already whole?"

"As long as we are attached to our Who or ego," Master Nomi responded, "we will always long for something, simply because the ego in and of itself is not complete. The Who keeps us from being whole. It fragments our lives. It cannot know its own spiritual awareness or experience its Zen. So it continually searches for ways to fill the void, which leaves it always in potential. Our happiness is unrealized and temporary instead of fulfilled and permanent. This seeking to fulfill itself could be through people, things, money, fame, or any 'thought' that fulfills your *happiness potential.* As I mentioned, in order to know where your Zen is, you must first see through the veil of the Who. Once this is achieved, one is free to *play* in life, as the moth who once knew its freedom and was able to dance in the wind."

Iill jumped in before Master Nomi could elaborate. "Our mind creates a web, and thus a pattern of our own ways of trying to survive. So unless we escape the web, we will only know the web or the pattern. And we will always think this web is our *only reality.* But if we journey outside of ourselves, so to speak, then we can enjoy pure freedom—the kind of freedom the moth knows. From there, as you say, we can 'play' in the world."

"I know this is true," Iill confessed, "because I've personally experienced being stuck most of my life. I've been trapped in a web of what I thought everything should be. I attempted to fill this void with things which never made me completely happy, or, as you say, *whole.*"

"Absolutely, mate," Mindful cheerfully agreed. "I know exactly what you're talking about. We all struggle with trying to get out of our own mental web so we can be happy and fulfilled. That's why we made this journey, aye?"

"Indeed," Spirit said. "I'm sorry to keep quoting Jesus, but it totally applies. *He who rules his spirit has won a greater victory than the taking of a city.* Ruling the spirit is knowing where your Zen is. That is to say, once we get outside the web of ourselves, we will become spiritually aware and re-learn how to play freely without the ego. That, indeed, would be even greater than the taking of a city."

Chapter 11:
Paradox Eight

As Master Nomi continued down the path, he offered this reflection: "The ancient masters knew that the web creates attachment, and such attachment was one of the great challenges of human-ity—that it is the root cause of our suffering. We become easily attached to many aspects of ourselves—our family, our work, our friends, our pets, our successes and failures, our habits—our very identity is trapped within all of these things. Once we learn how to escape the trap of attachment, we are free to *play*. Even when we do not get something we wanted, we will still remain happy and content. Finally, this means that our real bliss is not conditional. It does not depend on attaining something outside of itself. And this is the 'real secret.'

"When we are free of the ego, we discover how to enjoy unconditional love, unconditional friendship, and unconditional compassion. This happens only when we remove our awareness from the web of ourselves. We need to un-stick ourselves from the sticky mental web of the Who." Master Nomi paused and looked at the three travelers. "With that said, we are ready for the Eighth Paradox:

WITH ATTACHMENT, WORK.
WITHOUT ATTACHMENT, PLAY.

"When we are stuck in the web," the Master continued. "We experience the so-called ups and downs of life. Each intersection of the web is a point of attachment for us. All those points are where we have placed a need, desire, expectation, motivation, or something that keeps us there. But we fail to realize that each time we do this, the web is sticky and can trap us—even though we may feel *at home* in the web like the spider does." He then paused and said, "The web provides a way for the spider to get food. Not unlike us, our mental web provides a way for us to get what we *think we need*. The web creates patterns of our behavior that make us feel comfortable and secure, and therefore binds us even further. The more we repeat the patterns, the more stuck we become."

"So as you said before," Iill said, trying to distill what he'd heard, "play is our intrinsic nature; it's the way our inner potential is fully realized in our actions and reactions. But if we cling to our attachments and get stuck in the web, we cannot realize our *full* potential. It's only when we experience true play that we perform at our optimum, right? This is the opposite of what I was taught and how I have lived. I went blindly after my desires and attachments and became consumed with the goal of achieving them, instead of just enjoying the *process*."

Now it made perfect sense to him. "And you're right," he continued. "The goals which I did not fulfill made me become unhappy and feel like a loser…and that's the paradox: the more attached I was to something, the harder I felt I needed to work for it, and the harder it was to give it up. Those things that I was not attached to, I could easily enjoy and see them more clearly for what they really were … and this is true even with our loved ones. I know from my past relationships that did not work and were painful that the attachment unconsciously made me superimpose qualities and fantasies on my girlfriends that never really existed. With my last girlfriend, I became painfully aware of who she really was when I finally let go of my attachment to her. We are more effective and see more clearly when we are not attached."

Master Nomi suddenly stopped in a small clearing where there were several large boulders. He placed the lantern to the side of the boulder nearest to him and positioned it so as to cast a dim light over the other boulders. Then he sat down and gestured for the others to join him. As they seated themselves, the lantern's low light barely illuminated their faces. The shadows it cast silhouetted everyone, making the four seem as if they'd vanished into the darkness.

"It is true," Master Nomi began, "we get stuck to our expectations which make us act as robots, mindlessly going about our daily chores and work, never realizing that we are trapped like the spider.

In order to be free like the moth, we must transcend this mental web and see the pure awareness which lies between the sticky threads of the mind."

"What is pure awareness?" Mindful asked.

"I know!" Spirit replied excitedly. "It's the true awareness that we can attain when we get out of the web of our mind—when we get out of the trap of the ego. And then we know where our Zen is! I'm sure of it. It is there that we may find our spiritual awareness and experience the oneness of the universe or God-consciousness. He who rules his spirit, right?"

"Yeah," Iill added. "But that's not easy. This pure awareness is the paradox of how we must let go of ourselves in order to know where our Zen is. We stop looking in order to know. We have to give up everything we are so we can 'see' through the illusion of this mental web we've created in our mind. In a way, we need to get out of the very thing we've created. That's tough. You're saying we need to free ourselves of our sticky mental web by practicing the Secrets of No Mind and applying the Ten Paradoxes to our life. But how long is this really going to take?"

"Time is not important here, and we really give up nothing; we merely free ourselves,"

Master Nomi assured them, as he sat amidst the shadows of the rocks. "By making time an issue, it too becomes an obstacle in your path. Instead, consider the many benefits that come from using this technique, such as relaxation, which brings about stress control, learning to love unconditionally, fostering ultimate compassion in your relationships, developing peak performance in mind and body, sharpening your focusing skills, increasing your ability to concentrate and, most important, bringing about detachment so you can live more mindfully—or less mindlessly—with others, including yourself."

"And that's what I'm looking for, Master Nomi," said Mindful. "Peak performance when I'm in the game. Through playin' the game I'll know where my Zen is, aye. After that, mate, I know the rest of it will fall into place."

Chapter 12:
Paradox Nine

Then Spirit wondered, "Why are we sitting here in the dark? With this misty fog and that light flickering over our faces, we look like ghosts sitting on boulders. It's a little spooky, Master Nomi."

"Why do you say spooky?" asked the Master. "Is it because you can no longer see everyone clearly? Or are you associating this experience with a memory of something that you thought was spooky? Your mental web is seducing your perception and thus leading it astray."

The Master paused before continuing. "When we transcend ourselves, we merge into pure awareness, which is the essence of all things. By doing this, the thinker of the thought no longer exists, and there is just the thought. There is nothing to be attached to, because awareness lies in the emptiness between the sticky threads of the web. Our thoughts get stuck on the threads very easily. The thinker of the thoughts is merely the mental web performing its normal duties. The thinker is the thoughts. As we practice No Mind, our awareness becomes less and less stuck in the mind's web, and we become free because we have transcended the thinker."

"This," he revealed, "is the Ninth Paradox:

THINK. THINK NOT.
THERE IS NO THINKER.

Spirit pondered this and offered, "Then what you're saying, Master Nomi, is that we need to realize that the thinker is really just our thoughts working in the mental web; that what we really *are* is the subtle space between it all." The Master nodded in agreement. Then Spirit continued. "The nothingness between the threads of the web is where our Zen is. I get it now! The more we keep looking in the mind's web for our Zen, the more we are consumed with the web—and what we *think is not* the web—the less we are in the present moment. The nothingness is the Now! That reminds me of something I read in the *Kabbalah: 'If I am not for myself, who will be for me? And if I am only for myself, what am I? And if not now, when?'* To me, this is basically questioning the concept of the 'I' as it relates to *selflessness versus selfishness,* to who and what we really are, and it tells us that the answer to change can only begin and end in the Now."

Master Nomi, still partially obscured in the shadows, responded. "It is said in the *Tao* that it is not the spokes of the wheel that make the wheel functional, but the emptiness of the hub which makes the wheel useful. Thus, *what is not* is what gives us our substance. And the only way to find 'what is not' is to see through *what is*."

"And that is why it seems so difficult," Iill asserted. "We constantly strive for *what is* and try to accumulate more and more; so then we become attached to more and more things. When in reality it is *what is not* that we need to look for. That is where our Zen is."

"So basically," Mindful said, "we practice *no-thought* so we can see what's in between the thoughts or even the beginning of the thoughts."

"This is what is called the *hua t'ou*," Master Nomi reminded them. "*Hua t'ou,* you'll recall, means the head of the thought. When we experience the mind before the thought, we see through the veil of the Who . . . the thinker. When we do this and look into the nothingness, all things are merged into a field of pure awareness. In the silence, in the shadows, the boundaries of *things* disappear; therefore, we see their true interconnectedness with the essential substance of the universe: our spiritual awareness. And that is what the emptiness is that lies between the sticky threads of the mind's web; it is essentially *everything* and *nothing* at the same time."

"Okay, so we thought that the answer was in the mental web, in our mind," Mindful concluded. "But it isn't. It is outside the mental web or between the threads of the web, as you say, and the thought and the thinker are part of the web. By learning No Mind or *no-thought*, we get past the web and see what is really there. As long as we stay in the web, we can only see the web. And we can't know where our Zen is."

"That is true," Master Nomi agreed. "But don't be attached to that idea either, because in your attachment you will have gotten yourself stuck back in the mental web. It is best to disregard all labels and just practice with no expectations. You will come to see that it is the doubt that comes from the 'thought' of the emptiness that becomes your ally—until one day the doubt suddenly explodes into 'knowing.' This doubt supplies the tension which removes the shadow or illusion of Who. Then and only then will you know where your Zen is. It is said, *as you fall into the great abyss of unknowing, you suddenly catch yourself.*"

"What is the doubt?" Iill wondered.

"It is the doubt of the Who," the Master replied. "It is the doubt we all have of the thinker as just an illusion. And, ultimately, the doubt of what you will find when you realize the emptiness between the threads of the web. This is the doubt of enlightenment, of knowing where your Zen is. We do not know yet what we will experience, so there is great doubt."

Master Nomi then stood up, looked around, picked up the lantern, and started back down the dark, misty trail that cut a narrow path through the pine trees. As the lantern swayed, its glow cast a ring of light around the Master.

"So we all have this doubt when we begin our journey," Iill suggested. "It is necessary and natural. Even though we feel we are the thinker and make our own decisions, we really are just subject to the automatic mechanisms of our mental web. For this reason, we are truly not free. I mean, even when we think we are 'willing' something, if we break it down, we often find that what we thought we were choosing, or willing, is just an aspect of what we have *learned* to choose. Our *free will* itself is not so free, then. Really, it is more like *free won't* versus *free will;* we can edit what has already been pre-chosen for us by our own mental web."

"Right! Right!" the Master concurred with delight. "As long as we are the thinker, we are not free. As long as we are trapped within the web of ourselves, we see everything as polarities…we see opposites everywhere. The *Tao* says, '*We cannot know beauty unless we know ugliness, we cannot know sadness without knowing happiness, we cannot know dark without first knowing light.*' As long as we *think* within the mental web, we are stuck in the discriminations we make of all Things. We will always see many different Things and not the essence of all Things. We need to understand that opposites are merely two sides of the same thing—interconnected and not separate."

The fog was lifting with the first glimpse of the morning light as Master Nomi led the three down the trail. The birds were just beginning to sing their songs in the trees, yet the trail remained dark and difficult to see.

"So that is what is meant by *seeing God in everything,*" Spirit said, "and actually experiencing God in everything is finally *experiencing* where your Zen is."

"Yes," Master Nomi replied, "when you see beyond the opposites, you see the God in everything."

"Well, then, it's like the old *'How do you see the glass: half full or half empty?'* scenario," Mindful ventured. "If you see it as half *empty,* you're pessimistic. If you see it as half *full*, you're optimistic. We are usually one or the other, another play of the opposites, or should I say *stuck* in the opposites, aye."

"That's like God and the devil, good and evil, heaven and hell," Spirit said. "We've learned to see everything like this—in opposites. By splitting things apart, we don't see that they're actually related. As you said, Master Nomi, they are interconnected, like two parts of a circle, not two ends of a line. This is why there is so much prejudice and alienation in the world. People only see surface differences and miss that we are all connected through our spiritual awareness, through God."

"We really need to evolve to this higher level of consciousness as a human race if we are to survive all the environmental, sociological, and techno-logical problems that confront us today," Spirit concluded, as she peered through the trees up to the sky. She felt content in that moment; focused and connected. And then she smiled.

"Opposites are only two sides of one reality," observed Master Nomi. "They are two aspects of the same thing, and so they are interconnected and as such cannot be separated. In our mind, opposites will always co-arise together, as they are codependent. Our mind's mental web, busy trying to categorize everything, separates things into their opposites—all the while missing that they have the same root."

The Master then stopped and looked toward a small clearing near the temple. He turned and approached the clearing, where there were large, brightly colored clay vases and clay pots arranged around the edge of a small gravel garden. He stopped in front of a large vase about half his height, looked inside, motioned to the others to look inside as well, and asked, "What do you see?"

"The vase is half full of water; I'm an optimist," Iill said, as he laughed out loud. "Probably from the rain, right? Or wait a minute... is that half *empty?*"

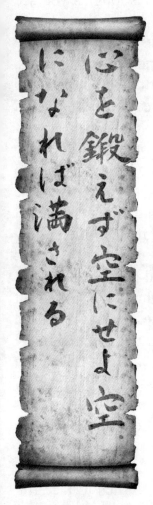
心を鍛えず空にせよ空になれば満される

Chapter 13:
Paradox Ten

Iill had no sooner spoken when Master Nomi came up from behind them with a thick bamboo stick. He took a swing at the vase and shouted, "Ai-*ya!*" The vase exploded into myriad pieces and the water splattered over the ground as Mindful, Iill and Spirit jumped back in surprise.

"Wow, Master Nomi!" Mindful exclaimed. "What are you doing? You're scaring me, again."

"Your mind is like the vase," the Master said as he looked down at the scattered pieces of clay. "It is *the vase* that creates the emptiness which can be filled. In the same way, its fullness creates its emptiness. As long as you see yourself as separate from the world around you, you always create the opposites; at the same time you create the categories and discriminations. Once you shatter this concept of Self—this *Who* we've spoken of—you will see the fullness and emptiness in everything, and you will no longer see the opposites. Remember, nothing is half empty or half full; it is the emptiness which gives rise to the fullness, and it is the fullness which gives rise to the emptiness. It is the boundaries of the vase, just like the boundaries of the mind, which allow you to see either. If you see it as one or the other, you fall prey to the illusion and miss the reality."

"I never thought of it like that," Iill said. "But it's true; I see it in my own life. I've always tried to fill the *feeling of emptiness* with something. I never really realize that I'm already full. I am only trying to fill the emptiness of the 'I' by constantly getting things I *think* I need—because, as you said, the 'I' can never be complete. And this is the illusion we all suffer."

"The world is formed from the potential of the void," Master Nomi said as he turned to face Iill, "like the tree from the potential of the seed; the *Tao* says it is better to see the source of all Things than to know the Things. We must learn to un-train the mind so, like the vase, we do not give rise to the emptiness which remains, in its pure potential, of being filled. Emptiness, by its very nature, seeks to be full; and fullness seeks to be empty. One is the other: we only know one because of the other. When we are *empty of ourselves*, only then can we see the fullness of the nothingness that is the universe. And so we arrive at the Tenth Paradox:

UNTRAIN THE MIND, BE EMPTY.
WHEN EMPTY, YOU ARE FULL.

Master Nomi bowed to each of them, then turned and walked toward the lanai where they had begun learning about the Paradoxes the night before.

Spirit reached out to the Master. "Wait!" she called. "How do we un-train the mind? How can I discover this fullness of emptiness and then know where my Zen is—experience the God in everything?"

"You have already briefly practiced the technique; you have been introduced to the Ten Paradoxes and some of the Secrets of No Mind," the Master replied. "Practice being mindful in everything you do, and you will discover the ultimate paradox of No Mind: *Awareness is the only universal constant.* That is how you discover your fullness in the emptiness. What underlies the essence of a flower underlies the essence of the galaxies and, thus, even the essence of a beetle."

The Master continued. "It is written in the *Tao* that having without possessing, acting without expectations, leading and not trying to control: *this* is the supreme virtue."

"Come inside," he smiled. "You will need to leave soon, as your driver will be here shortly. It is morning." He stepped onto the lanai and then into the main hall where the Ten Paradoxes hung on the wall and the stone lay on the table. The others followed.

"How did you know our driver would be here soon?" Iill asked.

"I'm so excited about what we've learned, Master Nomi," Spirit interrupted. "I feel energized, even though we've been up all night. But how can I learn more? May we come back and stay with you longer to practice?"

The group eagerly awaited Master Nomi's reply. He looked at each of them before he spoke.

"Take what you have learned and try to integrate it into your lives. We will need at least four weeks together the next time to go through the comprehensive understanding behind the Secrets of No Mind and the Ten Paradoxes. The Hut of the Blind Donkey will always be open to you all."

"I meant to ask you," said Ill. "What does the Hut of the Blind Donkey mean?"

"I will explain when you return to study further," Master Nomi replied. Then the four of them walked down into the dimly lit corridor which displayed the painted pictures illustrating the ox and its seeker.

The three took a closer look at the nine circular mandalas that resembled an ancient compass. Mindful noticed that one of them was like the image carved into the stone that lay upon Master Nomi's table. Spirit thought that the series seemed to suggest an expanding of awareness toward enlightenment—the realization of one's true nature.

"What are these circular images under the other pictures with the ox?" she wondered.

"One of these images was detailed into the ancient stone," replied the Master. "And I was able to interpret the symbol by using what is called the ancient ten oxherding pictures—they

are now almost a thousand years old. They represent the path of enlightenment depicted by a boy who seeks to know where his Zen is, as you all have called it, which is represented by the ox. He first finds the ox, and then chases it until he finally learns to master it. But he comes to realize that he and the ox are the same; and so they transcend their own boundaries, and he finally experiences where his Zen is. This is enlightenment."

"I will explain these in greater detail when you return," he added. "The mandalas represent my long effort to decipher the image on the stone that I found almost a quarter century ago. By discovering a corresponding link I found in the oxherding pictures, I was able to decode the ancient meaning of the stone. Of course, we will discuss this more in time. Let us hurry. I think I hear your driver approaching."

Master Nomi then gestured toward the door, opened it, and walked to the old gate at the street's edge. Mindful, Iill, and Spirit seemed hesitant to leave.

Mindful turned to the Master. "Well, Master Nomi," he said, "it was great to have spent this amazing evening with you. Your wisdom will forever have a special place in my heart. I hope to see you soon to complete this unbelievable journey. I now believe I have taken the first step."

Spirit, with tears of joy on her face, rushed to the Master's side and offered him a big hug. "Master Nomi," she said, her voice filled with gratitude, "I now see that there is indeed an actual *path*. And I think I have finally found the answer to 'Where's my Zen?' . . . or, at least, know that where it is, is where I *don't* look for it. Thank you from the bottom of my heart. I will return as soon as I can to continue the journey with you. I will practice the technique and apply the Ten Paradoxes whenever I can." She released him and moved away, her head bowed.

Iill then approached Master Nomi and said, "When I tell the folks back home about what happened here, they'll think I went off the deep end. But when I share the Ten Paradoxes, they too will see that the wisdom contained within them is accessible to everyone. I will create similar pictures in English of the Ten Paradoxes and place them in my office and conference room as guide-lines to remind me of the *Right Attitude* in life. I hope to follow the path and return here also. I wish you well, Master Nomi. Again, I thank you for everything and...*nothing*." With this last remark, Iill smiled as he caught Master Nomi smiling too, because he knew that he was beginning to understand.

Suddenly a new bus came up the hill and stopped next to the broken-down bus that had brought the travelers here the day before. The driver hopped out, appearing to be in a rush. He stopped, bowed to Master Nomi, and turned to the travelers. "Hey guys, I see you met Master Nomi. Sorry, but it took me a little longer than I expected to get back here." The three just looked at each other, astounded that the driver knew Master Nomi, and then they shook their heads and smiled at the Master.

"I had to wait for the company to send another bus this morning. But let's go! We can still make your destination on time today."

Master Nomi smiled back at the three. "There are many paths to continue your journey of experiencing where your Zen is, yet each path eventually ends at the same place. Remember, wherever you look, it is already gone," he said, and bowed to each of them as, one by one, they boarded the bus. As they headed down the road, the three waved until they were out of sight. The Master turned and disappeared behind the ancient wooden gate.

The Journey Continues . . .

Continue the journey with Master Nomi and get the second book in the series: the comprehensive 794-page book called *The Ten Paradoxes* which documents (with over 650 scientific, medical, psychological, and philosophical references) how the practice of No Mind® will actually *un-train* your thinking and teach you how to achieve Total Mental Fitness® by transcending the very structure of the brain.

The program demonstrates how to perform better, increase creativity, and become more intuitive in business, sports, relationships, spiritual awareness, and stress management. *The Ten Paradoxes* uses a technique clinically proven by top university and medical centers to have lasting benefits by reducing stress, enabling peak performance, alleviating or eliminating behavioral and psychological problems, and overcoming obsessive-compulsive disorders. How is it possible?

Self-Directed Neuroplasticity is becoming a well-known result of Mental Training as confirmed in recent neuroimaging studies.

The science and research of neuroplasiticity—the ability of the brain to rewire itself—reveal that through the practice of the No Mind technique, the brain can heal, change, and renew itself. Studies of Buddhist monks who use the practice of mindfulness have demonstrated remarkable changes in the patterns of the brain as seen through neuroimaging techniques.

Transcending the ego and changing our perception

As long as we live in a dualistic reality, we keep searching for what we think will complete us: material objects, relationships, achievements, spirituality, etc. But by practicing the techniques of the No Mind® program you become free from the limitations of your perceptual and ego defense mechanisms. These mental training techniques allow you to control your thoughts and desires, which you will come to know simply as objects of the mind. You will respond to a new open set of categories—ultimately learning to *act without trying*. This happens only when we are in harmony with our essential nature, which is the essence of nature itself.

When we transcend the automatic limitations and illusions of the "I," we develop insight and intuition that we can apply to enhance all aspects of our daily lives. And we can truly be in control of our destiny, decisions, and responses, without the overwhelming emotions we normally face, such as fear, worry, anxiety, prejudice, and greed. Thus, the achievement of Total Mental Fitness® not only allows us to break free of our automatic actions, reactions, and perceptions, it gives us the ability to make maximum use of our abilities through realization that *Awareness is the Only Universal Constant.*^{tm}

For anyone interested in advancing to the next level and learning more of the No Mind program, Master Nomi advises you to complete the steps outlined in the comprehensive program: *The Ten Paradoxes.* Go to www.wheresmyzen.com for more information.

Insight to Enlightenment

Finally pure awareness remains
I am exists nowhere
All Things endlessly change
A journey back to the Origin
Yet, enlightenment requires no voyage
Pure equanimity remains
Emotions dissipated
Intellections seized
Thoughts observed
As boats on a calm sea;
As though blind and deaf
Seeing with no eyes
Hearing with no ears
Mechanisms of perception immobilized
Ideas of holiness vanished
All Things belong to emptiness
Everything is understood as it is
Yet, enlightenment comes from what is Not

(For the continuation of this No Mind Insight see No Mind 601 in *The Ten Paradoxes* by Master Nomi)